Glasgow's East End in the 70s
from Gallowgate and London Road to Parkhead and Camlachie

Peter Mortimer & Duncan McCallum

MacLennan Arch looking towards Charlotte Street.

Stenlake Publishing Ltd

© 2014 Peter Mortimer & Duncan McCallum
First Published in the United Kingdom, 2014
Stenlake Publishing Limited
54-58 Mill Square, Catrine, KA5 6RD
www.stenlake.co.uk

ISBN 9781840336832

Printed by
P2D Books, 1 Newlands Rd,
Westoning, Bedford, MK45 5LD

Acknowledgements

Many thanks to everyone who encouraged us to produce this book, also Norrie McNamee, John Gorevan and Wull McArthur.

Further Reading

Gordon Adams – *A History of Bridgeton and Dalmarnock*
Willie Barr – *Discovering Glasgow*
Joe Fisher – *The Glasgow Encyclopedia*
Glasgow City Council – *Bridgeton Heritage Trail*
Glasgow City Council – *Calton Heritage Trail*
Andrew Heron & Andrew Wale – *Historical Directory to Glasgow Presbytery*
Hugh Mackintosh – *Origin and History of Glasgow Streets*
Senex – *Glasgow Past and Present*

WEBPAGES
www.architectureglasgow.co.uk
www.scottisharchitects.org.uk
www.oldglasgowpubs.co.uk
www.theglasgowstory.co.uk

The Georgian villa at 52 Charlotte Street.

Introduction

Lacking the glamour of other parts of Glasgow, the East End has never been pretentious, it readily acknowledges its working class roots. This lack of glamour however does not mask its rich social and industrial history, which Duncan McCallum managed to capture, as he photographed the streets of Calton, Bridgeton, Dalmarnock, Parkhead and Camlachie during the early 1970s. In the past couple of years, much of the East End has undergone major change, as the city has prepared to host the Commonwealth Games. This book hopefully provides a visual record of much what has been lost in the in the past forty or so years.

This view of London Road looking west towards Glasgow Cross has changed little since the photo was taken in April 1973, with the wedge shaped tenement on the right hand side the only structure to fall victim to demolition. Along with Gallowgate, London Road forms the second prong leading east from Glasgow Cross. Laid out in the 1820s, it runs out to Mount Vernon, so is a candidate as the longest 'road' in Glasgow. It has been known along its various portions as London Street, Great Hamilton Street and Canning Street, before being branded as London Road along its entire length.

Looking east on London Road, on the left hand side the waist high railing overlooks St. Andrew's Lane which ran off Gallowgate. The elevated walkway on the east side of St. Andrew's Lane was known as Schipka Pass, and took its name from the Battle of Schipka Pass, which took place in 1877 in Bulgaria between the Russian and Ottoman Empires. All the buildings east of St. Andrew's Lane as far as Moir Street have since been demolished and in 2014 the site became a small park.

This magnificent building stood at 35 to 41 Moir Street and 117 to 121 London Road. Spread over four storeys with an attic area, it commanded an excellent view of the area. Had this tenement survived, the flats would have been selling at the top end of the housing market. The ground floor is occupied by D O Stevenson, who specialised in bathroom suites. It was later to become the premises of the 'Mad Buyer', a shop that dealt in all manner of second-hand goods.

This is the south west corner of Charlotte Street and London Road, previously known as Stepney Place. The word 'Stepney' is still visible on the stonework, just to the left of the first floor window on the splay corner. One floor up, an elderly lady appears to content herself with a bit of 'windae hingin' which was and still is a popular pastime with Glasgow tenement dwellers. There has been a public house on this site since 1843, which in recent times was known as The Braemar and Fletchers.

At the latter end of the 18th century Charlotte Street was one of Glasgow's most desirable addresses. It was named after Queen Charlotte, consort of King George 3rd and grandmother to Queen Victoria. On its west side were four handsome villas, built around 1780. This example at No. 52 is the last remaining structure. To the right is a low rise tenement with a pend leading through to workshops in the back court area.

This view of Charlotte Street looking south shows some interesting architectural contrasts. The high rise flats of Hutchesontown from the 1960s, overlook the 18th century MacLennan Arch, which could be described as Glasgow's most mobile structure. It was built as part of the Assembly Rooms in Ingram Street and was initially located at the junction of London Road and Monteith Row. It then moved to the foot of Charlotte Street, as seen here. It now stands opposite the High Court on Glasgow Green. The older villa on the right hand side dates from the 1780s, and is typical in its design to others that once stood in the street, notably the dwelling of David Dale, which stood on the same side at No. 76. It later became the Eye Infirmary, then a Salvation Army Home before demolition to make way for Our Lady and St. Francis School which can also be seen further down the street.

Looking west along London Road in 1973 with the spire of St. Andrew's Parish Church rising majestically above the area. Just to the right of the Nags Head runs Charlotte Lane. The Nags Head dated from 1854 and was also known as the Railway Vaults. The low rise wall next to the pub conceals an air shaft for the rail tracks that run beneath. Within the row of shops on the right hand side are the premises of Glickman's, a company founded in 1903 who still make sweets and cough drops to this day from their shop. The billboard offers the new Austin Allegro.

The west side of Greendyke Street at its junction with London Road. The white building closest to Glasgow Green is the premises of R. Paterson & Son, who manufactured Camp Coffee; the smell of the manufacturing process often lingered around the area. The coffee essence was sold in distinctive glass bottles with a label depicting British soldiers serving in India. Next to Paterson's works is St. Alphonsus' School. In former times this area was known as Merkdaily, so named as the annual rent for the land was 365 merks Scots. Plans were once laid out here to build a grand development which was to be known as St. James Square, but the scheme never reached fruition.

Much of this scene remains unaltered today. The large building dominating the right hand side is the Hide and Tallow Market, built in 1890 for Robert Ramsay & Co. to a design by the architect John Keppie, who was a colleague of Charles Rennie Mackintosh. To the left of the market building is St. Andrew's Episcopal Church was built in 1752 and sometimes referred to as St.-Andrew's-by-the-Green. It was also known as the 'Whistlin' Kirk' on account of the organ that was played during services. This sort of thing was frowned upon by the Presbyterian churches of the day. The building is believed to be the oldest surviving Episcopal church in Scotland but in 1988 it underwent conversion into offices.

Looking across the footbridge is Humane Society House which was built in 1937 and replaced an earlier structure which dated from 1790. The Humane Society exists to save persons in distress in the River Clyde, and often had the grizzly task of recovering drowned victims from the water. Many Glaswegians will remember Ben Parsonage, who served as the Humane Society Officer from 1932 until his death in 1979, when he was succeeded by his son George. As a well respected citizen of the city, Ben had Parsonage Square in the Merchant City named after him.

St. Andrew's Footbridge was completed in 1855 and replaced an earlier ferry. It was designed by Neil Robson and built in wrought iron. An important pedestrian crossing, it links Hutchesontown with Calton and Bridgeton. In the background is the ornate UCBS bakery, which at its peak employed over 2,000 workers. The local Calton street gang 'The Tongs' appear to have marked their territory on the bridge pillar, probably in defiance of the Gorbals based 'Cumbie' gang. The high rise flats at Caledonia Road lurk in the background.

Above: Looking south down Moffat Street from Ballater Street, the view is dominated by the St. Mungo Halls, built in 1905. This popular venue was owned by the SCWS and frequently hosted concerts, weddings and socials, with the catering often provided by the nearby UCBS bakery in McNeil Street. Just beyond, are the workshop and stables, built in 1897 to a design by Bruce & Hay for the UCBS. In later years they became the garage repair works for bakery delivery vans. The site is now occupied by a housing development. The school railings of Hayfield Primary School are visible towards the Rutherglen Road junction.

Right The ornate central façade of the St. Mungo Halls.

Greenhead House dates from 1846 and was built for Glasgow cotton mill owner Duncan McPhail, to a design by Charles Wilson, who is perhaps best known for the Park development in the west of the city. In 1859 the building became the Buchanan Institute and provided education and training for destitute boys. The carved figure from 1873, seen on the left, depicts a boy studying and is known as 'The Mathematician', and acknowledges the former use of Greenhead House. It was further developed in 1904 and 1913, and later became Greenview Special School and St. Aiden's R.C. School. In 1906 it was converted into flats.

This attractive tenement block at 97 to 113 Greenhead Street, known as King's Park Place, dates from 1866 the oldest surviving tenement in Bridgeton, it commands a fine view over Glasgow Green. Beyond Tullis Street, on the left, a second identical block at Nos. 117 to 147 dates from 1865, completing the development. The ornate stone balustrade emphasises the quality of the tenement, one of the best of its kind in the district.

The dairy at the corner of Tullis Street and Greenhead Street is decked out with adverts for various products including Wall's ice cream, Players No. 6 cigarettes and Solripe soft drinks, which were made by Joseph Dunn (Bottlers) Ltd., at nearby Blackfaulds Place. Directly below the wall-head chimney are windows at each floor level which are not glazed. The 'urban myth' that they were bricked up to escape a window tax has a much more mundane explanation. Behind them lies the chimney vents or 'lums', which lead to the chimney at roof level. The dummy windows were included to retain the symmetrical appearance of the building.

The corner of Greenhead Street and Mill Street.

This tenement at 283 Greenhead Street has fallen into disrepair and is set for demolition. It is a good example of how the refurbishment programme of the late 1970s and early 1980s of tenemental properties in Glasgow happened too late for many fine buildings. In the background to the right hand side is Rutherglen Bridge, which dates from 1896 and replaced the original bridge from 1775, designed by James Watt. It was this bridge which gave the district its name, originally Bridgetown, later known as Bridgeton. For many locals it will forever be 'Brigton'.

The former grandeur of Monteith Row seems lost by 1976. It was laid out in 1819 and named after Henry Monteith, a cotton mill owner and Lord Provost of the city. It was one of the most desirable addresses in Glasgow in the 1820s and 30s, and the residents resisted the extension of London Road running along the front of their properties towards Bridgeton Cross, resulting in it being realigned behind Monteith Row.

The Monteith Hotel was opened at 14 Monteith Row in 1950 and provided accommodation for working men with the capacity for 60 residents. Around this time there was very little provision for adult men seeking housing, as families would have taken priority, so low budget options like the Monteith Hotel proved popular. It is the last remaining structure of the old Monteith Row.

This property at 15 and 16 Monteith Row, at the Morris Place corner was sub let by owners, who used factors to manage the tenants. This particular building was, according to the 1913 Valuation Roll, under the care of W C Faulds, House Factors at 133 Great Hamilton Street (London Road). Had the tenement refurbishment programme in Glasgow of the early 1980s been implemented sooner, then perhaps this attractive structure would still be with us today.

During its heyday Monteith Row was very much a desirable address in Glasgow circles. The 1913 Valuation Roll reveals that No. 25, at the corner with Morris Place, was occupied by Dr. John P. Granger a surgeon while next door at No. 27 was the dwelling of architect Robert Miller, emphasising the professional nature of residents in the area at that time. By the early 1970s both properties were multi-occupant as the area went into decline.

Situated at the east corner of Bain Street and London Road was Gillespie United Free Church, built in 1845. By the early 1970s when this photograph was taken, the church was in commercial use, occupied by the firm of B. Stern Ltd., upholstering manufacturers. Stencilled on the wall of the adjacent tenement is a sign for Matthew Riddell, wrights and contractors, wrights being an old term for what we know today as a building or joinery contractor.

St. James' Burgh Church at 212 London Road dated from 1816 and remained a place of worship until 1949, when it united with Pollok St. Aiden's. By the 1970s it was the premises of Glenalden Plastics. Occupied next door by Scottish Saw Services was the former St. James' School, which was relocated to a new building at Green Street in 1895. It later became the church hall for the adjacent church.

Looking south from Claythorn Street, the domed roof of the People's Palace is visible in the background. On the left graffiti tarnishes the wall of the Bankier Street corner, named after Robert Bankier, one of only four Provosts of the Burgh of Calton. The district was once the thriving community of many handloom weavers, and a stand alone burgh from 1817 until 1846, when it became part of Glasgow, as the city annexed many surrounding areas, as part of a municipal reorganisation.

Facing page upper: The dilapidated tenements at the corner of Claythorn Street and Moncur Street make for a rather depressing scene as the two women, wrapped up against the January weather, go about their business. The tenements in the vicinity replaced the rows and cottages that were prevalent in Calton during the 19th century. At nearby Calton Cross (junction of Well Street and Stevenson Street) stood a weaving college, where the skills of the trade could be passed on down the generations.

Occupying the corner of London Road and Claythorn Street was the former St. Luke's U.F. Church, built in 1849. Like other places of worship in the area, declining attendances forced closure, with the buildings being taken over by various businesses. In this instance the wholesale produce merchant, Wm. Murray has occupied the premises. A sight not seen so often nowadays is the lone dog wandering the streets unattended.

An everyday scene of London Road in the summer of 1973 with people going about their business. This portion of London Road was originally known as Great Hamilton Street, having been laid out in 1813 on top of a lane known as The Pleasants. The land here rose to a hillock around 15ft high, but levelled out as Great Hamilton Street extended eastwards, where it was known as Canning Street as far as Bridgeton Cross.

The classic Glasgow 'combo' on London Road, The Calton Bar and City Bookmakers, where a few pints of beer can be enjoyed whilst a bet on a horse or greyhound is placed next door. The buildings pre-date the tenements in the area and are a throwback to the times when Calton was a weaving village. The close at 391 London Road sports a dormer window arrangement at roof level, quite an unusual feature for a tenement in Glasgow.

Facing page upper: The Craignestock Mansions in the foreground were clearly built as a superior design of tenement, indicated by the attractive balustrade at roof level. Tenement builders often put commercial premises on the ground floor, as they yielded better rent. This building is named after a steading called Craignestock, which stood in the vicinity in the 18th century, before the Calton district was developed with houses and factories. It is built on the site of a previous tavern called the Old Herb Beer House and has undergone some name changes over the years, having been variously known as The Nationalist, The International Bar, The Weavers Inn and the Calton Bar.

Facing page lower: During the 1960s and 70s many churches in Glasgow became commercial premises. The McMillan & Calton Church suffered the same fate. Furniture Express Delivery Service, or FEDS as they appear to be known, operated from this London Road / Binnie Place location. The old Glasgow adage of main streets having a pub on every corner appears alive and kicking in this photograph. To the left is Meiklejohn's and the Ascot Bar on sentry duty at Craignestock Place. No. 436 London Road has the unusual, though not unique, feature of having windows on the gable elevation.

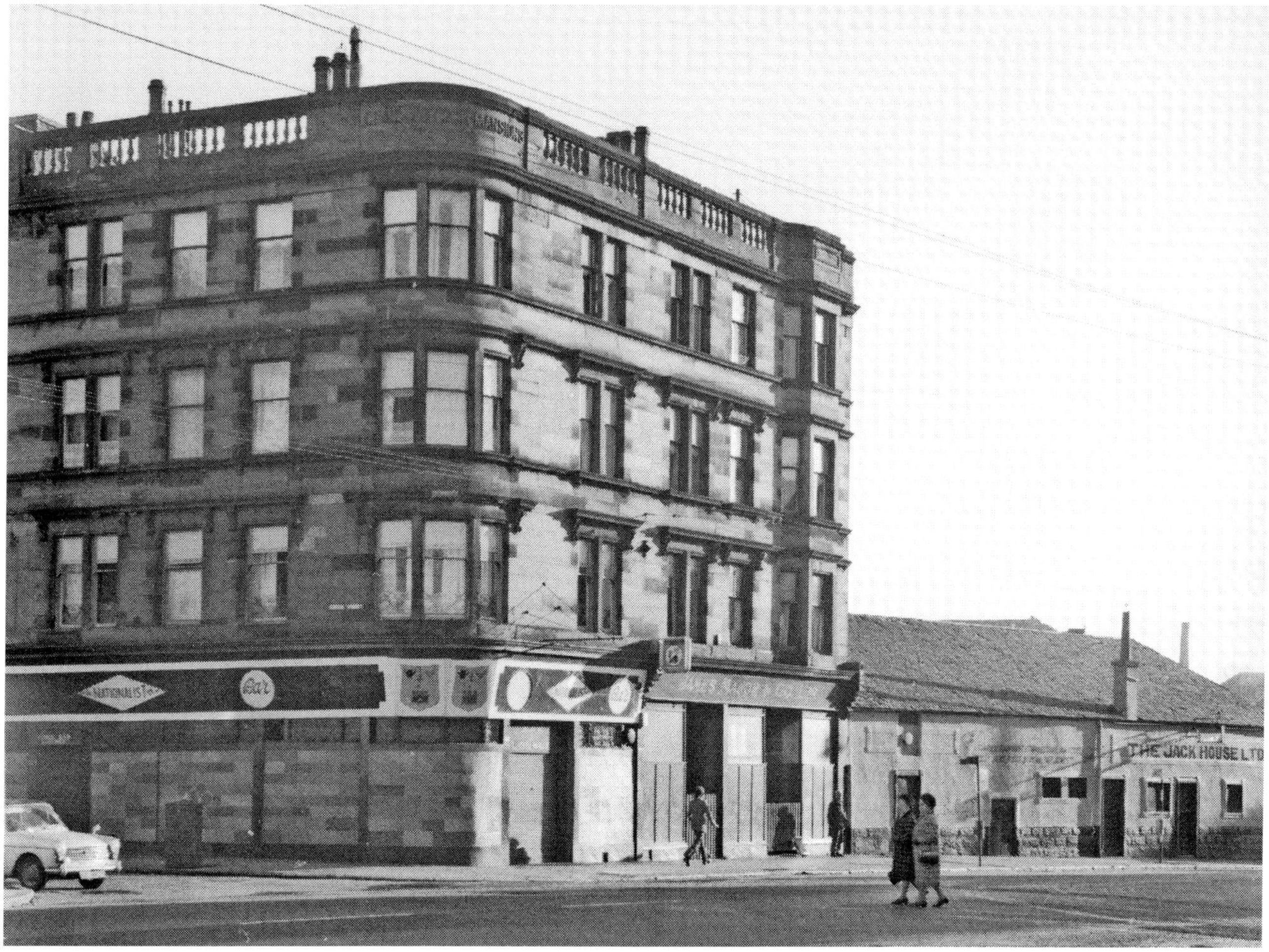
NATIONALIST
THE JACK HOUSE LTD

SERVICE
STORERS.
REMOVERS.

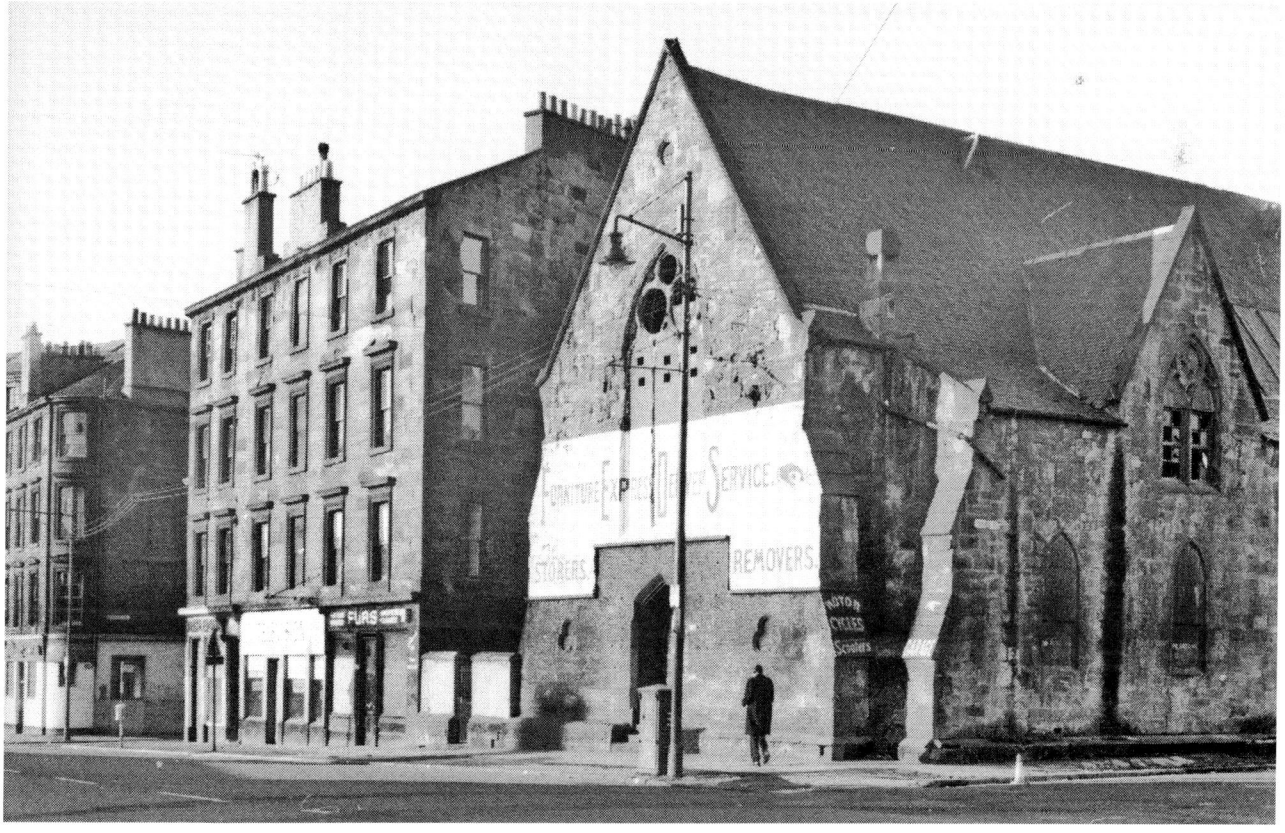

Tenement dwellings at 105 Arcadia Street dated from the 1890s and their construction was overseen by A. B. McDonald the City Engineer. This type of property was seen as very progressive in its day, with access gained from the rear by stairs leading on to balconies. The white painted building on the right was previously occupied by Film Transport Services Ltd.

At the junction of London Road and Blackfaulds Place was Slowey's public house. There had been licensed premises on the site from 1863, with the Slowey family acting as 'mine host' from 1934. Blackfaulds Place led into the Greenhead Brewery, which dated from 1800, when Robert Struthers, who became a Provost of Calton, began brewing ale. It later became the premises of Dunn & Moore. The billboard occupying a plum spot on the tenement gable offers Embassy Gold cigarettes, complete with coupons, which could be saved and redeemed for goods.

Looking east from Abercromby Street along Stevenson Street. It was named after Nathaniel Stevenson who had been Provost of Calton in 1826, in the days before it was part of Glasgow. It has been variously named in the past, Kent Street to Bain Street was called Russell Street, Bain Street to Well Street was New Street, Well Street to Green Street was Kirk Street and Green Street to Abercrombie Street was Stevenson Street. Clearly some rationalisation was needed and the whole thoroughfare became known as Stevenson Street.

This tenement at the corner of Abercromby Street and Stevenson Street bears the logo of the Glasgow City Educational Endowment Board, who were established under the auspices of the Education Endowment (Scotland) Act of 1882. It was the job of their commissioners to regulate the administration of funds left for educational purposes. It would appear that they chose to invest in the building boom of the late 19th century, earning rental income from the property. The railings at eaves level are indicative of a drying green positioned on the roof, as the building had a tight footprint on the corner of both streets.

Facing page upper: The workshop premises of glazing contractor Frederick Sedding share a frontage on Abercromby Street with the Grove Loan Co. who advertise at first floor level that they offer 'money advanced on all articles of value at low rate of interest'. To the right hand side the rear elevation of St. Mary's School on Forbes Street is visible. Abercromby Street is named after General Sir Ralph Abercromby, who fought in the Seven Years War and Napoleon in Egypt. It was previously known as Witch Lone and was reputedly the route taken by stonemasons living in Rutherglen, making their way to Glasgow Cathedral.

Facing page lower: The Fourways pub marks the busy junction of Gallowgate with Abercromby Street to the south and Bellgrove Street leading north. The premises of grocer and provisions supplier Henry Healy paint their offers on the walls and windows of their premises at 542 Gallowgate, which was a main shopping centre for housewives in the district.

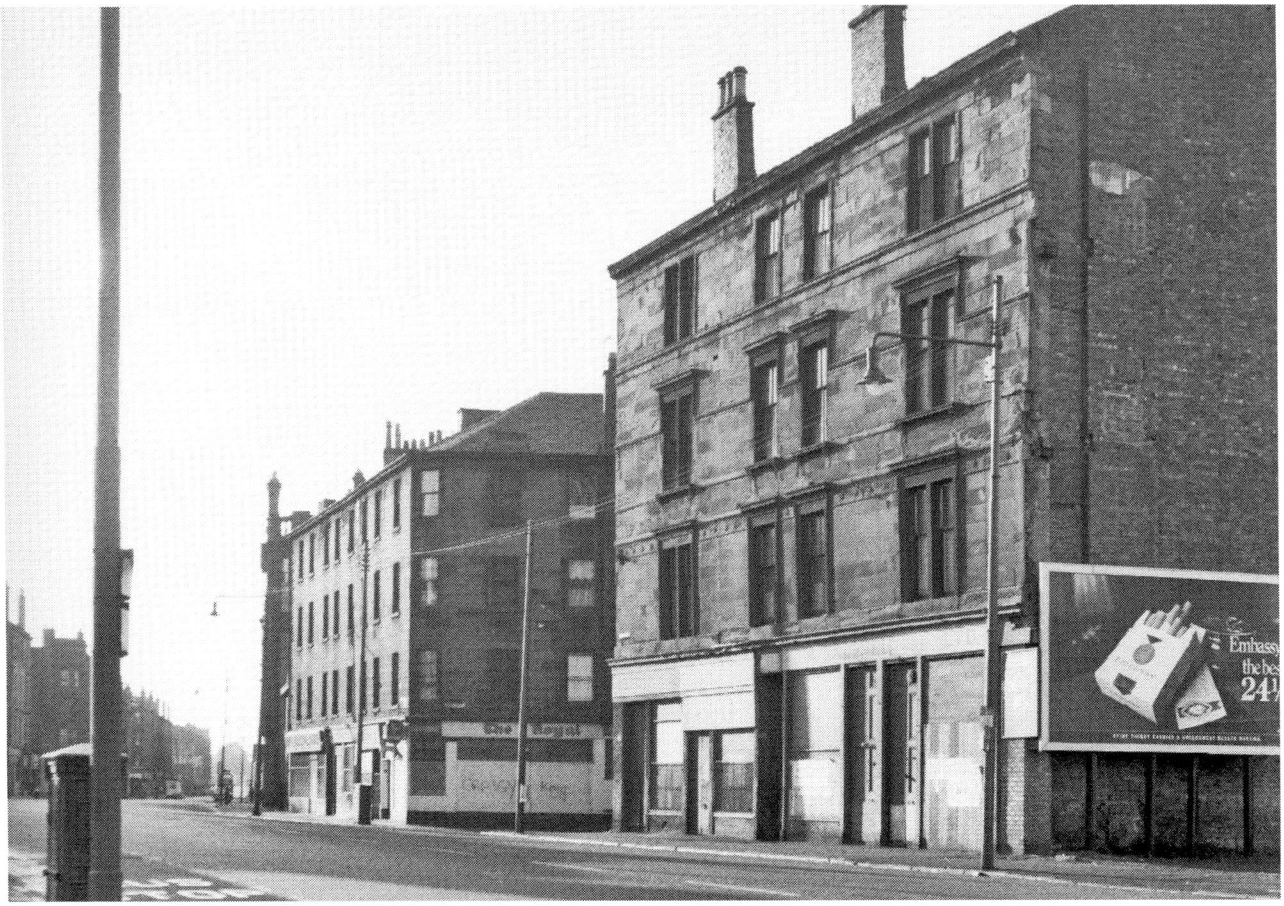
Embassy

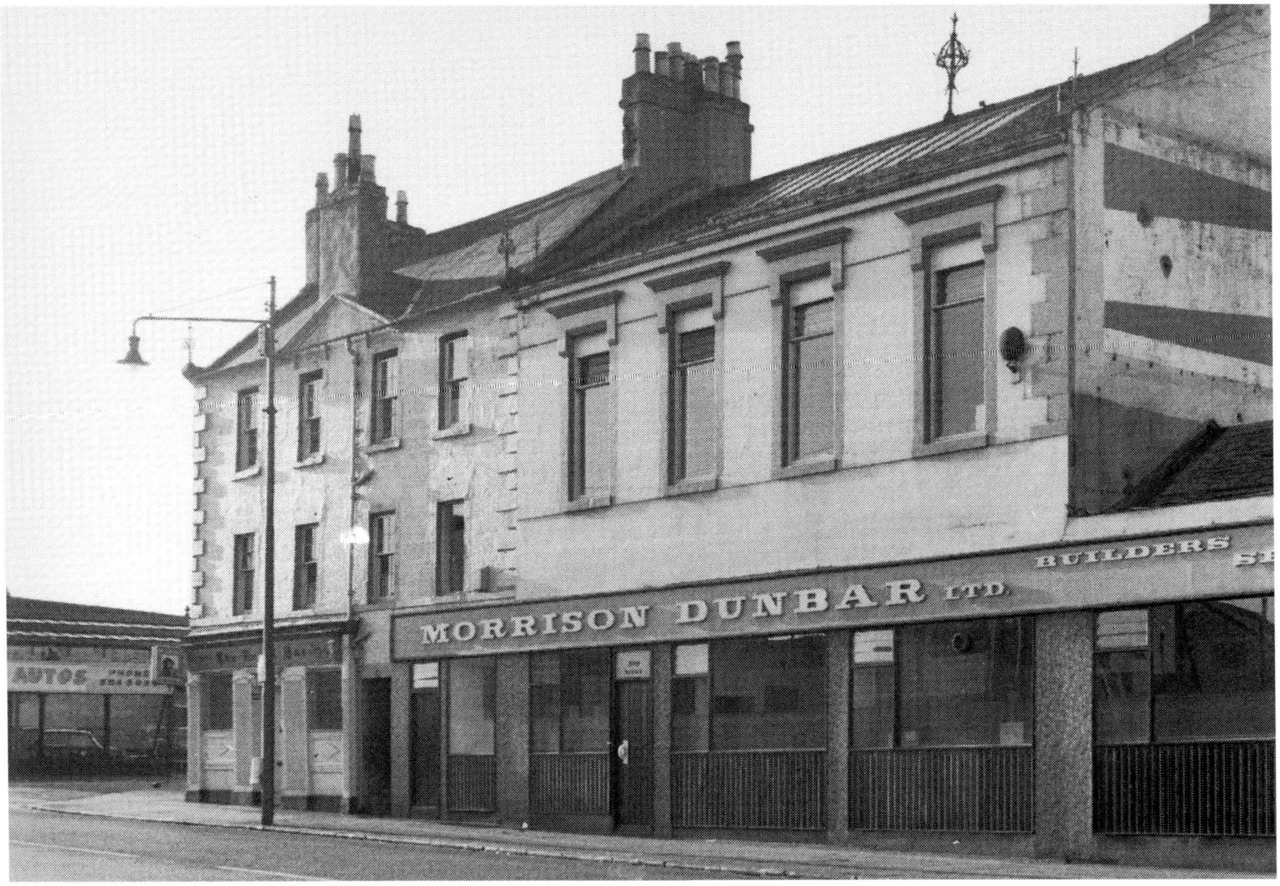
MORRISON DUNBAR LTD.
BUILDERS
AUTOS

Facing page upper: An unusually deserted view of the normally bustling Gallowgate looking east from Sydney Street. The north side Gallowgate at this point was originally known as the East Common or Gallowmuir, where executions were believed to have taken place in former times.

Facing page lower: The 1771 tenement at the west corner of Gallowgate and Claythorn Street is occupied on the ground floor by the Regal public house. Today it is known as the Heilan' Jessie and there are two versions of why it is so named. The first is that Jessie was a barmaid in a local hostelry frequented by soldiers from the Gallowgate Barracks, which stood opposite. The other account is that 'Helian Jessie' was the wife of a soldier from the barracks, accompanying him to India during the Sepoy Mutiny, and during the siege of Lucknow 'Jessie heard the sound of the Pipes, she rallied the exhausted defenders, the siege was over'.

The building with the 'Hire Drive' sign is an old tenement, one of a pair dating from 1771 that still stand both sides of the Gallowgate and Claythorn Street junction. They both predate Glasgow Barracks which stood opposite on Gallowgate and existed from 1795 until the 1870s, when the land was acquired by the railways and a new barracks was opened at Maryhill. To its left is the entrance to the garage, which was L shaped and ran behind the tenement. It was owned by James B. Rolinson Ltd., motor engineers, whilst a few doors along, on the extreme left of the photograph stands the Poltalloch public house.

The brick built factory of William White & Son at 42 Bain Street dates from 1877, built in an Italianate style to a design by Matthew Forsyth. Complementing Glasgow's tobacco production, the company was founded on the site in 1824 manufacturing clay pipes and by 1890 was making over 14,000 pipes per day which were shipped throughout the UK and all over the world. The business closed in 1951 and the premises became a mix of commercial premises, in recent years becoming part of the Barras street market.

East Campbell Street was laid out in 1784 and named after James Campbell, a tanner from Dovehill. The imposing building with the ornate balustrade is the U.P. Church, built in 1864 to a design by Haig & Low, replacing an earlier house of worship dating from 1792. The building is now occupied by the Lodging House Mission, providing support and accommodation for homeless and vulnerable persons. Just beyond, towards Gallowgate, is the Saracen Tool Works, premises of Alexander Mathieson & Sons Ltd.

Gallowgate was an important shopping thoroughfare in the east end, captured in this early morning view looking east from Little Dovehill. Gall's and High Walk Shoe Company were well known around the city, with their respective premises separated by a pend, known as Cumberland Court, which led to the Cumberland Foundry. The billboard on the tenement gable, close to Ross Street, encourages drinkers to try Carlsberg Special Brew.

The white painted building at 107 Gallowgate is the premises of The White Tower, who advertise a 5 minute service on their fish suppers, usually being served with bread and butter and a pot of tea. Adjacent, in Spoutmouth, is the Loch Erne public house, where licensed premises had existed on the site since the 1860s. Further east at 167 to 179 Gallowgate is the attractive four storey high Melior Building, with Reeta's Fashions occupying the ground floor. The ladies outfitters were established in the early 1950s and still trade from the same premises.

By 1976 the former White Tower fish restaurant had become the Happiness Chinese Restaurant, reflecting the changing palate of Glaswegians around that time. The gap site just beyond is faced off with an advertising hoarding, which reveals ads from the Salvation Army, British bacon and eggs, and Mini cars, which were very in vogue at the time following 'The Italian Job' movie.

Viewed from Charlotte Street, demolition workers have erected scaffolding at numbers 137 to 147 Gallowgate as they prepare to salvage materials from the condemned tenement. A demolition worker is visible working in the back court through the pend. The back-lands of many tenements in the city had small factories or works located there, with access for horses and carts to carry goods being gained by a passageway through the tenement, known as a pend.

Some local Calton worthies take in the demolition of Nos. 137 to 147 Gallowgate. The tenements were stripped bare by the demolition gangs, who would salvage slate, timber joists, fireplaces etc. for resale, before the wrecker's ball finished off the building. The man in the centre of the shot is very dapper, sporting a smart three piece suit, shirt, tie and raincoat, whilst gesturing to his seated colleagues, who are enjoying some heat off the bonfire in the backcourt.

The view looking east along Bell Street at the Spoutmouth junction, is overcast by the railway bridge heading north. The cobbled surface still remains, although the tenement is now the site of a car park, serving the edge of the city centre. Dovehill Primary School completes the view.

Dovehill Primary School was built in 1877 and was reputedly the first school in Glasgow to have showers for pupils. Following the Education (Scotland) Act in 1872, when it became compulsory for all children aged between 5 and 13 to be educated, there was a programme of building schools in the city, and by 1880 new schools were opened in the East End of Glasgow at Barrowfield (1875), Thomson Street (1875), Wellshot (1875) and Camlachie (1876).

There had been licensed premises on this site at 151 Duke Street from 1851, for a long time known as the Auld Gushet Hoose, later Jack's Bar. A gushet is an old Scots word for a triangular piece of ground, which in this case was formed by Duke Street and Parkhouse Lane. Above the pub were the premises of the Calton Loan Company, a firm of pawnbrokers. The stonework of the building had deteriorated quite badly, and demolition of the property was to follow within a couple of years.

The wall on the left hand side is the northern boundary of the College Goods Yard, looking west along Duke Street into George Street. The low rise building on the right is The Lampost public house also known as Carrs, which had a lamp-post in the middle of the pub as a feature. The tenements on the north side of Duke Street at the High Street junction were built as a consequence of the City Improvement Trust, established in 1866 to rid the city of its old vennels and closes, to be replaced with sandstone tenements.

Looking south down John Knox Street, ahead is the impressive bulk of the Great Eastern Hotel. Originally built as a cotton mill in 1849 for the firm of R.F. Alexander, the five storey high structure took on plenty of daylight for the workers through its numerous windows. In 1907 it was converted into a hotel and could accommodate up to 450 persons, but in later years was used by men of modest means. Running alongside the western gable of the building is the Molendinar Burn. The tenements on the left hand side are perhaps more reminiscent of those found in Edinburgh, rather than the common plain fronted version often found in working class areas of Glasgow. The pend through the building showing 'Garage' originally led to the works of Lewis & Co., furniture manufacturers.

The tenement at 48 to 58 John Knox Street is dwarfed by the new high rise across the street on the Ladywell development, which was completed in the mid 1960s, on the former site of Duke Street Prison, which closed in 1958. In the background the high rise developments in the Gorbals complete the backdrop.

These tenements at numbers 57 to 79 John Knox Street overlook the cradle of Glasgow. Wishart Street is laid out on the line of the Molendinar Gorge, where St. Mungo established a church in the 6th century. The Molendinar Burn, flows from Hogganfield Loch, winds its way along the west gable of the Great Eastern Hotel, and is culverted through St. Andrew's Square, spilling into the River Clyde near the High Court at Saltmarket. In the background the Royal Infirmary completes the scene.

The tenement run at numbers 6 to 34 Glenfield Street awaits the inevitable fate of demolition which has already claimed the opposite side of the street. At right angles is 57 Alexandra Parade which is already derelict during the wholesale revamping of the area. Glenfield Street was to disappear under the extension of the Royal Infirmary, replaced with the Queen Elizabeth building.

Firpark Terrace sits high above Ark Lane, overlooking Dennistoun. The close furthest down the slope at No. 2, was once the home address of Charles Rennie Mackintosh. He was born in 1868 at Parson Street in Townhead before moving here. He was to become one of Glasgow's most famous sons and established a world wide reputation as an architect and designer. The son of a Glasgow policeman, Mackintosh married Margaret McDonald. Along with her sister Frances and her husband Herbert McNair, they became known as 'The Four'. They had a distinctive style of design which has been much copied in the modern day, on everything from the simple tea towel to expensive jewellery.

This is a view looking south down Dunchattan Street from Broompark Drive captures the last days of this particular corner of Dennistoun. This area was laid out on the lands of Dunchattan, which were owned by Charles MacIntosh, who set up a dye works in 1777 which manufactured cudbear, which was a dyeing powder extracted from lichens. He reputedly built a high wall around his works to keep his operation private. He also employed only Gaelic speaking workers from the Highlands so that they could not tell people on the outside what was happening in the works. His son, also called Charles, developed the process of waterproofing fabrics, and from him we have the Mackintosh raincoat.

These tenements at 49 to 73 Edmund Street appear to have been vacated and await demolition. The general store, or corner shop would have serviced the needs of the now gone population. Just beyond the last close is the wall and railings of the long gone children's playground. At the top of the hill tenements in Cardross Street remain occupied, having been refurbished and stone cleaned, and now form an impressive sight from nearby Duke Street, as they line the route up to Golfhill.

This view looking south down Westercraigs is dominated by Blackfriars Parish Church, completed in 1877 to a design by Campbell Douglas & Sellars. The parish was originally located at Blackfriars Street in the Merchant City and could trace its origins back to 1622. The parish operated out of Dennistoun until 1982 and a few years later the building was converted into housing. Further down is a row of tenements once known as Kings Cross Place, the name being taken from the junction of Duke Street, Bellgrove Street and Westercraigs which was Kings Cross. There was a fashion in Victorian Glasgow of calling streets and places after London thoroughfares. Other examples of London names being copied in the city includes Charing Cross, Picadilly Street and Cheapside Street.

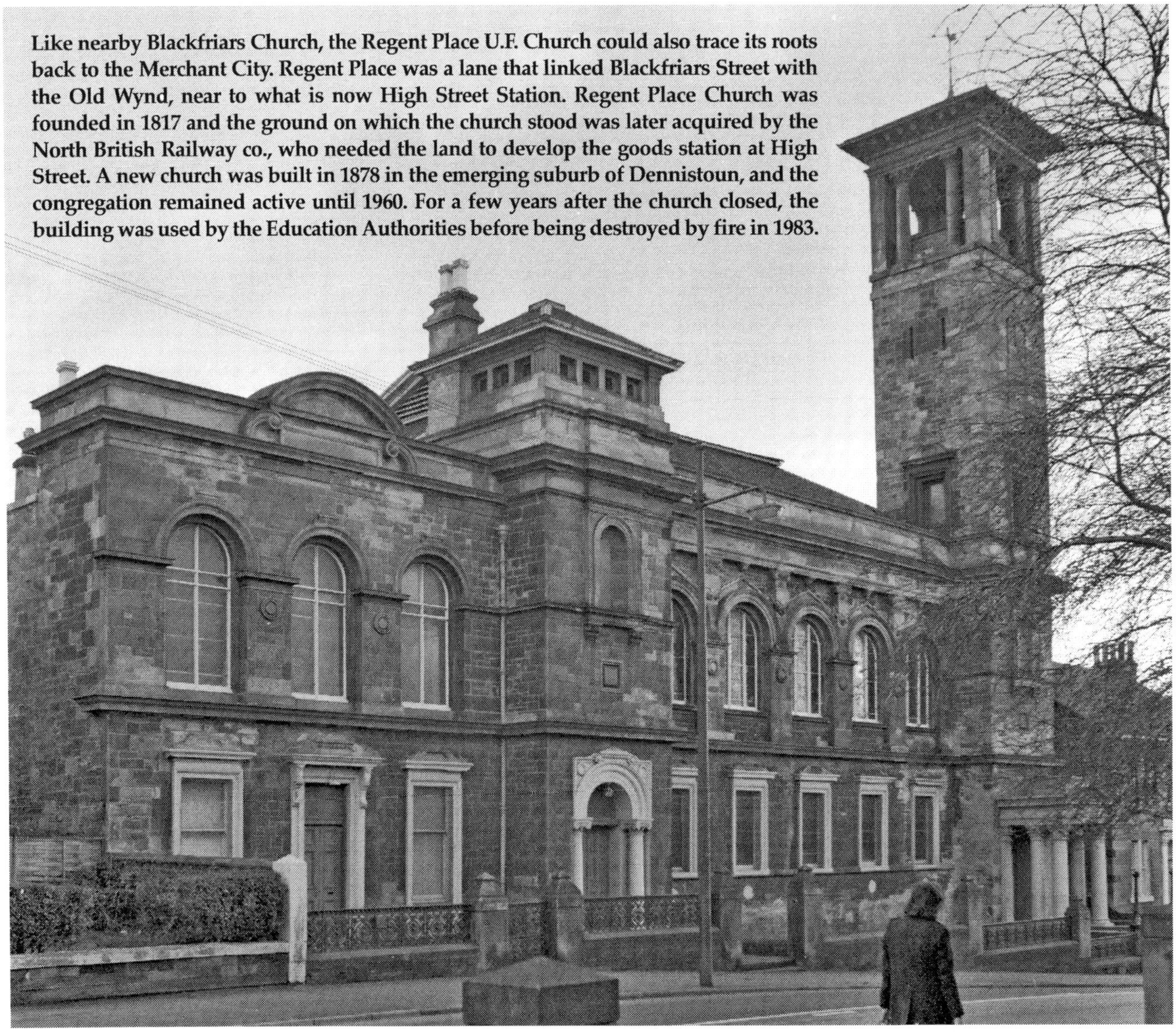

Like nearby Blackfriars Church, the Regent Place U.F. Church could also trace its roots back to the Merchant City. Regent Place was a lane that linked Blackfriars Street with the Old Wynd, near to what is now High Street Station. Regent Place Church was founded in 1817 and the ground on which the church stood was later acquired by the North British Railway co., who needed the land to develop the goods station at High Street. A new church was built in 1878 in the emerging suburb of Dennistoun, and the congregation remained active until 1960. For a few years after the church closed, the building was used by the Education Authorities before being destroyed by fire in 1983.

This railway footbridge spanning the Bellgrove East Junction on the Glasgow to Airdrie rail line, continues to provide a useful link from Bellfield Street off Gallowgate, over to Dennistoun. The other options for those on foot are Sword Street and Millerston Street. The woman on the bridge appears to be suitably dressed for the cold January day, as she returns home with her shopping, or as it would be known around the city, her 'messages'.

Looking east along Wellpark Street, the former Wellpark Institute dominates the view. It was built in 1867 as a Free Church School providing education to locals, among them the children of brewery workers from the nearby Wellpark Brewery. It closed in 1959 and lay derelict and vandalised for many years before being completely refurbished in 1996, and now plays home to the Glasgow Building Preservation Trust. To the right hand side we see the wall of the Meat Market, which opened in 1875 at nearby Moore Street. An abattoir was added in 1911 along with cattle pens. The boy and girl in the foreground seem oblivious to their surroundings as they enjoy a game of street football.

The north end of Sydney Street near to Duke Street provides a good example of industry and housing comfortably sharing the same street. Tenements occupy the footprint from Wellpark Street northwards, whilst at the other corner the brick building with the vented roof dates from 1908 and was built as stables and sheep pens for Brechin Brothers, butchers. The site was ideally placed for the nearby meat market, which dominated this part of Calton.

Facing page upper: On the west side of Sydney Street are tenements at Nos. 3 to 23. Note the pend at No. 21, which led into the rear of the property, whilst the Wee Man's public house occupies the corner with Gallowgate. There had been licensed premises on this site from the early 1800s, whilst across the street, on the corner with Lambert Street, the Old Canteen Bar could be traced back to 1847.

Facing page lower: On this view looking south-west on Orr Street, visible at nearby Kerr Street is the Broomward Carpet Works, occupied by Thomas Graham & Sons, plumbers merchants. The works were built as two separate entities, firstly the Broomward Mill, Cotton which dated from 1867, and secondly the Broomward Cotton Works, built in 1915. Both facilities were acquired by James Templeton & Co, who also had nearby works at Glasgow Green. In the foreground is the Crofters public house and the stone railway bridge crossing the lines coming out of Bridgeton Central Station. Orr Street is named after John Orr, a Glasgow merchant who owned Barrowfield Estate. The upper portion of the street was once known as Marlborough Street and Henrietta Street.

The brand stamp of P. & W. MacLellan confirms the date of 1890 on the railway bridge at Kerr Street in Bridgeton. It was built for Bridgeton Central Station which opened for passengers in 1892, with the line connecting through to Gallowgate Central at Lambert Street. P. & W. MacLellan were formed in 1832 and established their Clutha Works at Kinning Park, and had MacLellan Street named after them.

The Christ Episcopal Church at the corner of Brook Street and Crownpoint Road built in 1835 to a design by John Henderson. It was a popular place of worship for soldiers from the barracks at Gallowgate. Attached is a Clergy House which dates from 1914, which was later used by the Social Work Department. The church has been demolished and the Clergy House is in a state of disrepair.

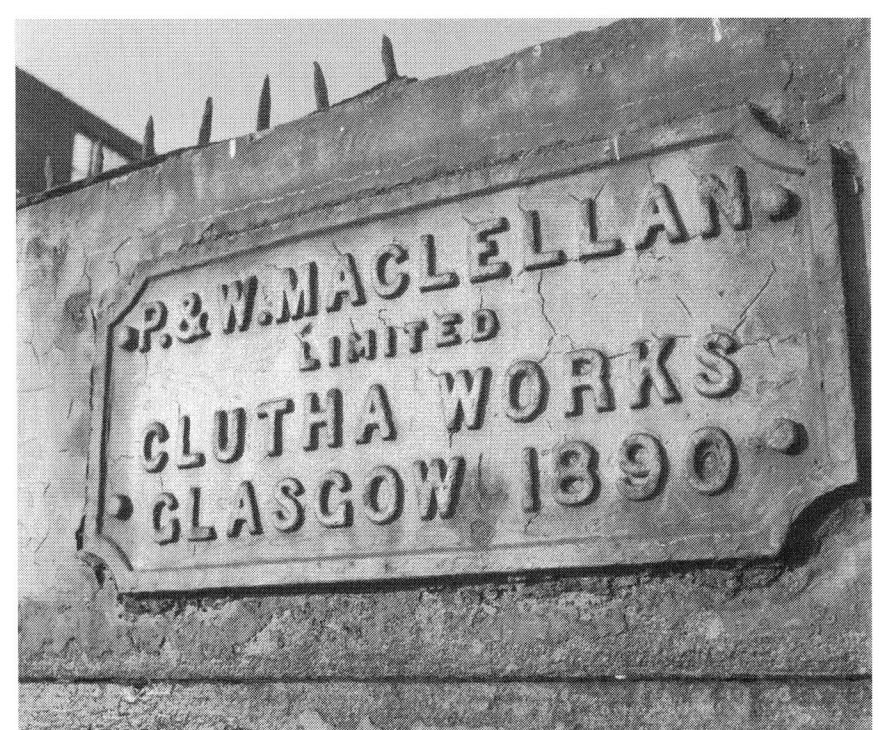

The corner of Broad Street and Orr Street in Mile End is dominated by a tenement awaiting demolition in early 1974. The International Bar on the ground floor is a large pub boasting a public bar and lounge. The more modest hostelry The Park Lane Tavern is visible at the eastern end of the block. The Leyland truck is owned by Andrew Smith, slaters and plasterers who had premises in Broad Street, whilst the Linwood built Hillman Imp completes the scene.

Worshippers at St. Thomas's can check the timings of various activities at the church on the sign above the entrance. Reflecting in the window of Neil & Machin, the image of the Orient Cinema on the opposite side of Gallowgate, can be seen. This low rise run of shops was once owned by The Eastern Co-operative Society with outlets for their butchery, grocery and bakery businesses. The platform shoes worn by the young woman walking along is in keeping with the fashion of the 1976 date when the photograph was taken.

Facing page upper: The plain structure of St. Thomas's Church at Wesleyan Street appears to await demolition in February 1976. The building dated from 1823 and was designed by John Baird, with alterations carried out in 1893 by Honeyman and Keppie. It later became St. Thomas's Wesleyan Methodist Church, with the street taking its name from it.

Facing page lower: This small factory, so typical of many in Glasgow at the time, was built in 1859 to a design by the architect William Baillie. Its original owners were William Riddell & Co., who were wireworkers, specialising in the manufacture of riddles, sieves, fireguards and ornamental garden wire work. The premises were later occupied by Alexander Gray, a tea merchant, before being acquired as the Bellgrove Grain Mills by Alexander Waddell. The 'implement merchants' signage on the right hand side, may be a relic of the William Riddell occupation of the works. The site is now covered by the Crownpoint Sports Centre.

The tenement block on the north side of Gallowgate at the junction with Fielden Street and Millerston Street was known as the Paterson Building. The low rise buildings further up Gallowgate to the right, mark the spot where Camlachie Mansion stood. It was here that General James Wolfe stayed on his visit to Glasgow. He gained fame when he captured Quebec from the French in 1759. The public house at the left hand corner acknowledges his connection with the district. The square chimney to the end of the tenement block belongs to the Crown Fireclay Works which lay just behind. The whole scene is now almost all part of the Forge Retail Park. The 62 bus to Hope Street, police box and gents toilet at the Camlachie Street junction complete the scene.

This view of Gallowgate looking east towards Parkhead Cross is taken from the gates of the Eastern Necropolis. It was laid out as a cemetery in 1847 on the lands of Little Tollcross, which were owned by Robert McNair and his wife Jean Holms, and nearby Janefield Street is named after her. In the centre of the photo is Invernairn Street with the Reekie Linn public house at the corner. William Beardmore who owned Parkhead Forge, took the title of Lord Invernairn when he was knighted.
Most of the area on the north side of Gallowgate is now taken up by the Forge Shopping Centre and cinema complex.

This tenement block at 1109 to 1123 Gallowgate is derelict but previously had a row of shops and business premises on the ground floor. The small children's playground would have proved popular with the children in the Camlachie area. Beyond this stands the Hartshead Works, dating from 1877 and extended in 1914 for Macrae & Drew, bedding manufacturers.

The clock tower of Camlachie Police Station fronts on to Yate Street, where workmen had fashioned a football boot, ball and goalposts into the cobbled surface of the street. To the left are the roofs of the warehouse buildings of Camlachie Distillery, which was established in the 1830s and produced whisky until 1923, after which it became a bonded warehouse. It was here that Polish soldiers were billeted during the Second World War. Both the police station and distillery have been demolished.

Looking east along Camlachie Street, in the centre foreground can be seen the back elevation of Camlachie Police Station, built in 1877 to a design by John Carrick, the City Engineer. The school roll at Newlands Primary School in Parkhead records some children as having their home address as 'Camlachie Police Station', indicating there was family accommodation in the building. It was demolished in 1980. Just beyond the police station is Camlachie Institute, which opened in May 1890 and was a centre for meetings, worship, concerts and pastimes. In the background is a railway viaduct over Gallowgate which was known locally as the 'Croft Bridge'. Just beyond the viaduct is the roof of Camlachie Primary School from 1876.

This view looking east at Parkhead Cross remains virtually identical today. To the right is Tollcross Road heading east, and Westmuir Street making its way towards Shettleston. The tenement at the splay corner between the two was built in 1905 to a design by J.C. McKellar. Parkhead began as a small weaving village, and was soon caught up in the mass industrialisation of the 19th century when the Reoch Brothers opened Parkhead Forge in 1837. William Beardmore acquired the works in the early 1860s and went on to build an industrial empire, much of it focused on Parkhead Forge. It closed in the early 1980s and the site is now the Forge Shopping Centre.

This tenement at the corner of Duke Street and Westmuir Street is known as the Watson Tenement, built in 1905 to a design by Crawford & Veitch. It is adorned with busts of the Watson family, who were wealthy local property owners. They lived at nearby Muiryfauld Drive, and family member James R Watson was a Professor of Chemistry, whilst George Watson was a merchant and victualler.

The Trustee Savings Bank Building was built in 1908 to a design by John Keppie, a contemporary of Charles Rennie Mackintosh. The sculpture at the top of the building signifies Prudence Strangling Want, which would have been most appropriate when the building was used as a bank, but perhaps less so, when it was later converted into a public house.

In this view of Burgher Street off Parkhead Cross the side elevation of the Glasgow Savings Bank building takes up the right hand side of the photograph. The bank was founded in 1836 and has undergone various changes of ownership in its history. Further along on the same side is the Sharpe Memorial Church, built in 1907 to a design by Hugh Campbell as Parkhead Pentecostal Church. It was the first building in the area to be lit by electricity. The Reverend George Sharpe raised money for the building project in North America, and an early teacher at the church was Miss Olive Winchester, heiress of the inventor of the Winchester Rifle. A new church was built on the site in 2014.

At No. 79 Westmuir Street stands Parkhead Congregational Church, built in 1879 to a design by Robert Baldie. To the left of the building runs Ravel Row, a name that takes us back to the weaving history of Parkhead in former times. To the right of the church is Craibs public house, later to become the Bonnie Prince Charlie.

Parkhead Primary School is comprised of two separate schools. The west side of the building is the former Parkhead Barony Sessional School, opened in 1868, and pre-dates the Education Act of 1873 which required all children aged between 5 and 13 to be educated. This resulted in local authorities embarking on a school building programme in the latter part of the 19th century. The eastern portion was built as Parkhead Primary School in 1879 to a design by Hugh MacLure, and was joined to the former by a covered walkway.

Lauries newsagent shop appears to be still doing good trade despite the obvious distress of the tenement run at 207 to 225 Westmuir Street. Further west, the gable end of 185 Westmuir Street provides a focal point for billboards promoting cigarettes and gin. The woman crossing the road, with her shopping or 'messages' as Glasgow likes to call them, sports sandals with platform heels which were in fashion at the time.

The tenement at the corner of Gallowgate and Duke Street, to the right of Tom Martin tailors, was built in 1902 to a design by Burnet, Boston & Carruthers on the site of George Henry Farmer's public house. The ground floor was occupied by the Clydesdale Bank, but has in more recent times been a tanning salon, perhaps reflecting modern tastes. The woman crossing Springfield Road in the foreground may well be making her way from Parkhead Washhouse, judging by her pram, which appears to be missing a child. The white van waiting for the traffic lights to change shows a telex number, which is probably now redundant in the new age of emails and websites.

The village of Parkhead was founded on coal mining and hand loom weaving. This old weaver's cottage at 886 Springfield Road was one of the last remnants of the old village. This type of cottage served as a home and a workshop, with all the family involved in the weaving trade. As industrialisation arrived in Parkhead, principally through William Beardmore's Parkhead Forge, the old weavers' cottages were replaced with more functional tenement buildings, to meet the needs of an entirely different population. In its latter days this cottage became a newsagent's shop, before being finally demolished.

London Road curves away from Bridgeton Cross with the tenements at Nos. 641 to 673 beginning to look the worse for wear. The top of the Bridgeton Cross Shelter is visible to the left. It was built in 1874 and manufactured and assembled by George Smith of the Sun Foundry at Port Dundas. A policeman in a white coat directs traffic around the Cross, where seven routes converge.

Bridgeton Cross Mansions date from 1896 and are the work of architect John Cunningham, notable for the 'onion dome' ventilator crowning the building. The tenements fronting on to Bridgeton Cross were in the main of a superior quality and still stand to the present day, with only the block on Main Street and James Street, which housed Logie's drapery store missing from the original layout.

Landressy Street runs from 598 London Road to Tullis Street and takes its name from the town of Landres in France, which was the home of Turkey-Red dye workers who came to Bridgeton to pass on their skills and knowledge to local weavers. The portion of the street shown, from London Road to James Street, was one of the busiest streets in the district. It had Bridgeton Workman's Club, established in 1865 and built here in 1897 to a design by John Gordon. Next door is Bridgeton Public Library, dating from 1906 by J. R. Rhind, a Masonic Hall from 1909. On the right is the Barrowfield West Church at 10 Landressy Street, built in 1868 as the Barrowfield Edgar Memorial. As attendances started to dwindle, combined with high running costs, in 1962 the congregation merged with Greenhead Church round the corner at 570 London Road. This section of Landressy Street also had the distinction of being the only street in Glasgow with a tram route at each end of the street (London Road and James Street). Only the library remains from the collection of public buildings.

Bridgeton Central Halls at the James Street and Landressy Street corner were built in 1926 with this unusual turret, almost mimicking the minaret of a mosque. The church was the home of the 155th Company of the Boys' Brigade. In 1964 the church closed, with the congregation merging with St. Thomas' Church at 760 Gallowgate, and the site is now occupied by a housing development. Beyond the Central Halls, the building with the flagpole is the Greenhead Weaving Factory, built in 1888 for Thomas Thomson, cloth manufacturers, and it also has since been converted into housing. The premises of Jupiter dry cleaners is just visible on the right.

The Bridgeton Burial Ground at Tullis Street opened in 1811 and was aligned with the Bridgeton Relief Church. It was here that the great and the humble of the district were interred and burials continued until around 1869. It was originally accessed via Landressy Place where there was a small gatehouse at one time. By the 1970s it had fallen into considerable disrepair. The building with the steep pitched roof and small gable chimney was at one time used by the YWCA. Tullis Street had originally been known as John Street and due to duplication of street names in the city was renamed after the local firm of John Tullis, whose St. Ann's Leather Works were situated on the street.

The White Hart was one of a dozen pubs on the landscape of Main Street from Bridgeton Cross down to the River Clyde. Corner sites were the most sought after by publicans, in the belief that increased their chances of attracting customers. The abandoned dairy premises are adorned with posters encouraging voters to back the local SNP candidate.

The shop occupied by Fontana Wine Company, licensed grocers, at 97 Main Street was a former doctor's surgery. To the left was a branch of the city wide grocery chain Galbraith's Stores, known for its hams, butter and cheeses to stock the larder of many a Glasgow family. The firm was established in 1894 and by the start of the Second World War had 159 stores, many of them situated in tenement blocks.

The circular corner of this tenement at the junction of Dalmarnock Road and Playfair Street maximises the limited space available. The close in Playfair Street was home to the pawnbroking firm of R & D Smith, and the bracket holding their sign, minus the traditional three brass balls can be seen jutting out on the Dalmarnock Road elevation. On the extreme left the Station Bar at the corner of Mordaunt Street is visible.

The low rise building at 93 to 101 Dalmarnock Road predated most of the tenements in the district, and was at one time owned by the British Cotton & Wool Dyers Association, reflecting the weaving trade carried on in Bridgeton and Dalmarnock. By the 1970s the ground floor had become the premises of HA Crombie, licensed grocers. Just beyond the taller tenement at 105 Dalmarnock Road is the frontage of Pirn Street.

The January sun in 1976 casts long shadows on Dalmarnock Road. The street cutting off to the left is Ruby Street, which was perhaps best known as the site of the Dalmarnock Tram Depot, the site of a major fire in 1961 which caused extensive damage. Further east at 197 Dalmarnock Road is the Dalmarnock Congregational Church. Nothing of this photograph remains.

Located at 231 Dalmarnock Road is the Dalmarnock Congregational Church, built in 1902 to a design by J C McKellar. It was home to the 175th Company of the Boys' Brigade and attracted boys from the district, who would attend meetings on a Friday night, play football for the Company on a Saturday afternoon, and attend church on a Sunday. This routine played an important part in keeping many boys and young men occupied, and often kept them out of trouble. As Glasgow became depopulated during the 1970s and 1980s the thriving community of B.B. companies diminished and many disbanded.

This stretch of tenements on the north side of Dalmarnock Road between Hozier and Ruby Streets is awaiting demolition. Already at Nos. 177 to 185 the slates have been stripped off the roof, probably for re-sale. The building housed a doctor's surgery on the ground floor, as well as a sale room, home bakery and Dot's fruit shop. A thoroughfare such as Dalmarnock Road would have shops of every sort to meet the needs of the local population, at a time before large supermarkets and shopping malls.

East End Sawmills were founded in 1951 by a local joiner called Robert Frew, supplying trade and DIY customers with their timber and ironmongery requirements, latterly from premises at 367 to 375 Dalmarnock Road. In the background the Millerfield high rise flats are visible, with the first of four being completed in 1964, and standing 23 storey high with 132 flats for tenants. By 2007 they had all been demolished by controlled explosion, and the site developed as the athletes' village for the 2014 Commonwealth Games held in the city.

In ancient times there was a ford across the River Clyde which could be crossed by wading through the water. The present Dalmarnock Bridge was completed in 1891, replacing earlier wooden bridges at the location from 1821 and 1848. In the background the premises of cleaning products manufacturer Sanmex are visible on the Rutherglen side of the bridge.

In the background stands Dalmarnock Power Station on the banks of the River Clyde. It was built by Glasgow Corporation Electricity Department to meet an increasing demand for power and became operational in 1920 and was further extended in 1935. It was coal fired and well placed to receive supplies, being positioned on the edge of the Lanarkshire coalfield. The People's Palace has in the past displayed aerial photographs taken by the Luftwaffe during the Second World War of the power station, as it was an obvious target for them. It was eventually demolished and the site is now vacant. The riverside path proves a popular haunt for local dog walkers.